Contents

Some words are printed in bold, **like this**. You can find out what they mean by looking in the glossary on page 30.

Who was Michelangelo?

Michelangelo is one of the greatest artists who ever lived. He was an all-round genius, who excelled at everything he did. Today, he is best known as a painter and as a **sculptor**, who carved beautiful figures. He was also a poet and an **architect**, who designed some great buildings.

Works of genius

Michelangelo was born in Italy in 1475 and lived until he was 88 years old. During his long life, he created many masterpieces. His most famous sculpture is the large statue of *David* made for the city of Florence in Italy. He also created an amazing set of paintings for the ceiling of the Sistine **Chapel** in Rome.

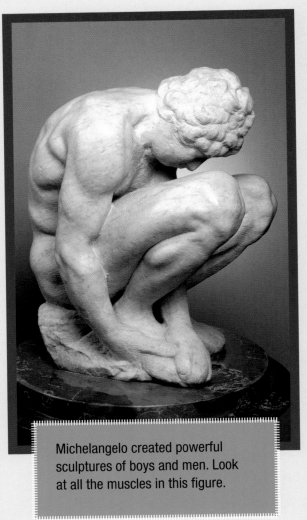

Michelangelo created powerful sculptures of boys and men. Look at all the muscles in this figure.

An emotional man

Michelangelo worked for some very important people, but his life was not easy. He was an emotional man with a fiery temper. His powerful personality made people react to him strongly. Some people loved him and others hated him.

CULTURE IN ACTION

Michelangelo

Jane Bingham

www.raintreepublishers.co.uk

Visit our website to find out more information about Raintree books.

To order:

☎ Phone 0845 6044371

🖹 Fax +44 (0) 1865 312263

🖥 Email myorders@raintreepublishers.co.uk

Customers from outside the UK please telephone +44 1865 312262

Raintree is an imprint of Capstone Global Library Limited, a company incorporated in England and Wales having its registered office at 7 Pilgrim Street, London, EC4V 6LB – Registered company number: 6695582

Text © Capstone Global Library Limited 2010
First published in hardback in 2010
Paperback edition first published in 2011

Edited by Louise Galpine, Rachel Howells, and Helen Cox
Designed by Kimberly Miracle and Betsy Wernert
Original illustrations © Capstone Global Library Ltd.
Illustrated by kja-artists.com
Picture research by Hannah Taylor and Kay Altwegg
Production by Alison Parsons
Originated by Dot Gradations Ltd.
Printed in China by CTPS.

ISBN 978 1 406212 08 2 (hardback)
14 13 12 11 10
10 9 8 7 6 5 4 3 2 1

ISBN 978 1 406212 28 0 (paperback)
14 13 12 11 10
10 9 8 7 6 5 4 3 2 1

British Library Cataloguing in Publication Data
Bingham, Jane
Michelangelo. – (Culture in Action)
709.2
A full catalogue record for this book is available from the British Library.

Acknowledgements

We would like to thank the following for permission to reproduce photographs: Alamy p. **19** (© Derek Croucher); istockphoto pp. **11** (maxphotography/ © Massimo Merlini), **15** (© lillisphotography), **20** (© Adrian Beesley), **24** (© sumbul); SuperStock p. **9** (© De Agostini); © SuperStock, Inc p. **14**; The Bridgeman Art Library pp. **4** (Hermitage, St. Petersburg, Russia), **5 top** (Vatican Museums and Galleries, Vatican City, Italy/ Alinari), **5 bottom** (Casa Buonarroti, Florence, Italy), **6** (Private Collection), **7** (Museo de Firenze Com'era, Florence, Italy / Alinari), **8** (Casa Buonarroti, Florence, Italy / Alinari), **10** (British Museum, London, UK), **12** (Church of San Domenico, Bologna, Italy), **16** (Gemaeldegalerie Alte Meister, Kassel, Germany / © Museumslandschaft Hessen Kassel Ute Brunzel), **18** (National Gallery, London, UK), **22** (Vatican Museums and Galleries, Vatican City, Italy, Alinari), **23** (Opera del Duomo, Florence, Italy, Alinari), **25** (Biblioteca Medicea-Laurenziana, Florence, Italy), **26** (Fogg Art Museum, Harvard University Art Museums, USA, Alpheus Hyatt and Friends of the Fogg Art Museum), **27 top** (Private Collection, Photo © Bonhams, London, UK), **27 bottom** (Private Collection).

Icon and banner images supplied by Shutterstock: © Alexander Lukin, © ornitopter, © Colorlife, and © David S. Rose.

Cover photograph of self-portrait of Michelangelo, reproduced with permission of Alamy (© Lebrecht Music & Arts Photo Library).

We would like to thank Susie Hodge, Jackie Murphy, and Nancy Harris for their invaluable help in the preparation of this book.

This painting is from the ceiling of the Sistine Chapel in Rome. Even though they are painted on a flat surface, the figures look **3-D** from below.

Broken nose

When Michelangelo was a teenager, another young sculptor punched him on the nose. He was jealous that Michelangelo was a better artist than he was. After that, Michelangelo hated the way he looked. He often tried to hide away from other people.

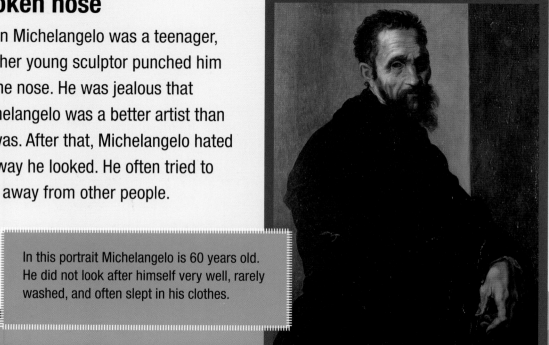

In this portrait Michelangelo is 60 years old. He did not look after himself very well, rarely washed, and often slept in his clothes.

Michelangelo's world

Today, Michelangelo is known simply by his first name, but his full name is Michelangelo di Lodovico Buonarroti Simoni. He lived from 1475 to 1564. For most of his life he worked in the cities of Florence and Rome, but he also travelled to other parts of Italy.

In Michelangelo's time, the cities of Italy were **independent** states. Florence was ruled by **merchants** (people who traded goods) and by bankers. Rome was controlled by the Pope, who was the head of the **Roman Catholic Church**.

Inspired by the past

Around 1350 an exciting new movement started in Florence. Artists, writers, and **architects** became very interested in the art of ancient Greece and Rome. They tried out new ideas, inspired by the past. This movement was later called the **Renaissance**, which means "rebirth". In the 1350s there was a rebirth of art, learning, and architecture in Italy.

This is a copy of a famous Roman statue of the Emperor Marcus Aurelius. Roman sculptures like this one inspired the artists of the Renaissance.

This painting shows Florence in Michelangelo's time. It was a wealthy city, with many grand houses and churches.

A brilliant time

In Michelangelo's time, there were some brilliant artists working in Italy. Leonardo da Vinci and Raphael both lived and worked at the same time as Michelangelo. The three great artists saw each other as rivals (people who competed against each other).

Leonardo da Vinci (1452–1519)

Like Michelangelo, Leonardo da Vinci had many talents. He was a painter, a **sculptor**, an architect, and a musician. Leonardo was an inventor, too. He designed many machines, including a type of helicopter.

Early years

Michelangelo spent his early years in a village outside Florence. His mother was often ill, so he was cared for by a stonecutter's wife. As a boy, Michelangelo watched the stonecutter use his tools to cut blocks of marble. He longed to be a **sculptor**, so he could carve beautiful statues out of marble.

Studying art

When Michelangelo was six years old, his mother died. He was a clever boy, and his father wanted him to train as a **merchant**. But Michelangelo had other ideas. He begged his father to let him work in an artist's **studio**.

At the age of 13, Michelangelo started work for the painter Domenico Ghirlandaio. For the next two years, he worked as an artist's apprentice (a young person who learns a trade). But he still dreamed of being a sculptor. He was thrilled when he was picked to join a special school for sculptors.

Michelangelo carved this marble **panel** when he was about 16 years old. It is called *The Madonna of the Stairs*.

A school in a palace

The sculpture school was held in the palace of the Medici family. The Medicis were very wealthy bankers who controlled the city of Florence. In the sculpture school, the students copied ancient sculpture. They also studied the writings of the Greeks and Romans.

This painting is by Ottavio Vannini (1585–1644). It shows Lorenzo de Medici with a group of students.

Lorenzo de Medici (1449—92)

Michelangelo became a favourite of Lorenzo de Medici. Lorenzo was the most powerful man in Florence, but he also loved books and art. He was Michelangelo's first **patron**. He paid Michelangelo to create works of art.

Studying the dead

When Michelangelo was 17, Lorenzo de Medici died. Without a patron to pay for his work, he could no longer work as a sculptor. Instead, he spent a lot of time in the hospital of Santo Spirito in Florence. The hospital was run by **monks** (holy men). The monks examined the bodies of the dead to help them find out more about diseases.

Michelangelo helped the monks to examine dead bodies. This taught him about anatomy (all the parts that make up the human body). Later, he used this knowledge in his art.

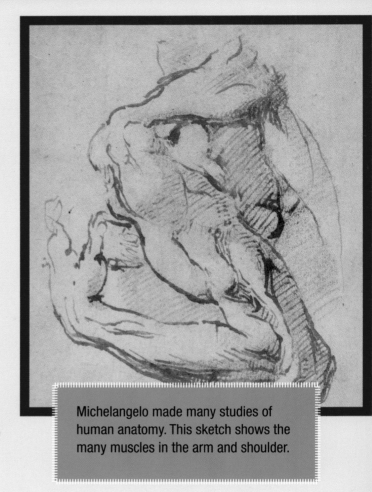

Michelangelo made many studies of human anatomy. This sketch shows the many muscles in the arm and shoulder.

Moving to Rome

Michelangelo's first big chance came when he was 21. He was called to Rome to work for a cardinal, a very important priest in the **Roman Catholic Church**.

The cardinal wanted a sculpture for the **tomb** where he would be buried after he died. The subject that he wanted was the *Pietà*. This was a religious scene in which Christ's mother, the Virgin Mary, holds her son's body after he has died.

A first masterpiece

Michelangelo finished the *Pietà* when he was about 24. It was carved from a single block of stone. People could not believe that such a young artist could produce such a masterpiece.

Signing the sash

Michelangelo's *Pietà* in Rome is the only work that he signed. There is a story that he wanted to prove that the sculpture really was his work. He crept into St. Peter's Church in the middle of the night and carved his name on Mary's sash.

This is Michelangelo's Rome *Pietà* (1497–99). In this sculpture, the figures look very young. It contrasts strongly with Michelangelo's later version of the *Pietà* (see page 23).

Carving a sculpture

Sculptors carve their figures using a hammer and chisel. They place the blade of their chisel on the stone. Then they use their hammer to bang on the end of the chisel. This drives the chisel blade into the stone, cutting out small flakes of stone.

Stone carving takes lots of practice. If you cut too deeply, it is very hard to put your mistake right. If you chip off a piece, such as a nose, the sculpture is ruined.

Using marble

Marble is especially hard to work with. Sometimes a piece of marble can develop a crack that causes the whole sculpture to break. Marble is expensive so sculptors cannot afford to make mistakes.

Michelangelo carved this angel from marble when he was just 20 years old.

Carve a soap sculpture

You can carve a simple sculpture from a bar of soap. Work carefully, carving off small pieces of soap, and be very careful with sharp sticks!

You will need:

- A cocktail stick
- An old ballpoint pen
- A potato peeler
- Some newspaper to spread under your work.

Steps to follow:

1. Use a cocktail stick to draw the eyes, nose, and mouth on your soap.

2. Then use a pen and the cocktail stick to carve out the features.

3. Use a potato peeler to carve your soap into the shape of a face, showing the cheeks, forehead, and chin.

If you wash the soap a few times with cool or lukewarm water, your carving will look much clearer and smoother.

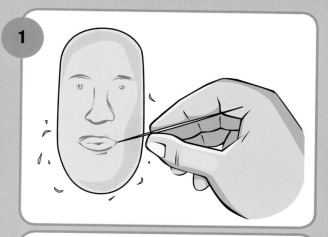

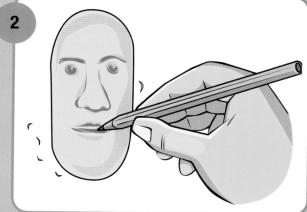

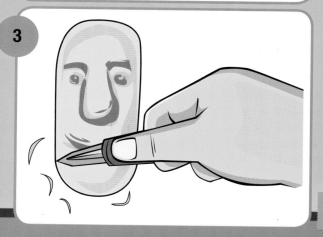

Creating *David*

In 1501, Michelangelo left Rome and went back to Florence. After the death of Lorenzo de Medici, there had been many troubles in the city, but now Florence was peaceful again.

The new rulers of Florence asked Michelangelo to make a statue for their city. The subject of the statue was the figure of David. He was a young hero in the Bible who defeated the giant Goliath.

Michelangelo's *David* was based on classical sculptures, but it was made on a much larger scale. The statue is over 5.17 metres (17 feet) high, almost three times as tall as a man.

The young *David* is frowning in **concentration**. This shows us a hero who thinks as well as acts.

A hero for Florence

The rulers of Florence thought that David was the perfect hero for their city. They admired David's courage in standing up to an enemy who was much bigger than him. This reminded them of the courageous people of Florence, who had faced some very powerful enemies.

Michelangelo's *David*

Michelangelo did not show David as a conquering warrior. Instead he showed the moment just before David fought Goliath. The figure of *David* is strong, but also calm and **dignified**. Michelangelo's statue has become one of the world's most famous works of art.

Did Michelangelo make a mistake?

David's head and hands seem too large for his body. But Michelangelo did not make a mistake. The statue was meant to be placed high up on a building. This meant Michelangelo had to carve a figure that would look good from below. Parts of *David's* body had to be bigger to make the **proportions** look correct.

The story of David and Goliath

In the Bible story, David and Goliath fight a terrifying battle. Goliath has a huge sword and he wears **armour** to protect his body. David has only his sling and a few stones.

At the start of the battle, Goliath attacks. He swings his sword and roars, but David keeps dodging out of the way. Then David takes careful aim with his sling – and hits the giant smack in the forehead!

Goliath falls to the ground with a terrible groan. David seizes the giant's sword and cuts off his head. Then David returns in victory to his people. Now that he has destroyed Goliath, they can all live in peace.

This painting by Caravaggio is called *David With The Head of Goliath*. It was painted 90 years after Michelangelo sculpted his *David*.

David and Goliath: the musical

Why not make your own musical version of David and Goliath? You could tell the story on page 16. Or you could tell a modern story about the triumph of the little guy.

You can create tunes by clapping and making sounds or you can use musical instruments. You could even stage a David and Goliath rap!

Steps to follow:

1. First compose two theme tunes, one for David, and one for Goliath. David's tune should feel light and lively. Goliath's music should sound heavy and frightening!

2. Now think about how you will create the battle scene in sound. The death of Goliath could be loud at first and then very quiet.

3. The last scene can show David returning in triumph. You can end with a loud version of his theme tune, showing that the little guy has won in the end!

The Pope's ceiling

In 1505, Pope Julius II invited Michelangelo to work for him. One of Michelangelo's first tasks was to paint the ceiling of the Sistine **Chapel**, in Rome. The chapel was a special place of worship inside the Vatican Palace, where the Pope lived.

A terrible task

Michelangelo did not want to paint the ceiling. He said he was a **sculptor**, not a painter. But the Pope insisted he must do it. Pope Julius was a moody and difficult man, but he was the head of the **Roman Catholic Church**. Michelangelo knew he must obey him.

For the next four years, Michelangelo worked full-time on the painting, but Pope Julius was very hard to please. He nagged Michelangelo all the time. Once he even hit him with a stick.

This painting shows Pope Julius II. It was created by Raphael in 1511–12.

Instant old age

Michelangelo was 33 years old when he started work on the Sistine Chapel ceiling. By the time he had finished, four years later, people said he looked like a haggard old man.

Scenes and figures

Michelangelo created a beautiful design for the Sistine Chapel ceiling. He painted a series of scenes that tell the Bible story of the creation of the world. In between the scenes are many large figures, sitting on thrones. They are prophets and sibyls, men and women who could tell the future. Altogether, there were more than 300 figures in Michelangelo's painting.

God's creation of Adam is the most famous scene from the Sistine Chapel ceiling. Look at the way the hands of God and man do not quite touch. Why do you think Michelangelo showed the hands like that?

Michelangelo had a vast area of ceiling to cover. It measured 40 metres by 14 metres (130 feet by 45 feet), which is close to the size of an Olympic swimming pool.

Painful positions

The hardest thing about painting a ceiling is that you have to paint above your head. Some painters lie flat on their backs. Others prefer to stand and lean backwards.

Michelangelo did not lie on his back. Sometimes, he painted standing up, with his head tipped back so he could see what he was doing. Sometimes he leaned on a wooden support with a ledge for his head. But whatever method he used, he always got covered in paint. He also suffered from terrible backache for the rest of his life.

ART ACTIVITY

Painting above your head

Why not try out different ways of painting above your head? It will help you understand how much Michelangelo suffered for his art.

Steps to follow:

1. First try Michelangelo's method. Stand with your arms above your head, and tip back your head. Then mime the actions of painting on a ceiling. How does it make you feel? Imagine you were Michelangelo, painting in that position for 12 hours a day!

2. Now try drawing a picture when you are lying on your back. Tape some paper to the underside of a table, and lie on some cushions to make you high enough. Use a wax crayon to draw your picture. Is it easy to draw? How does this position make you feel?

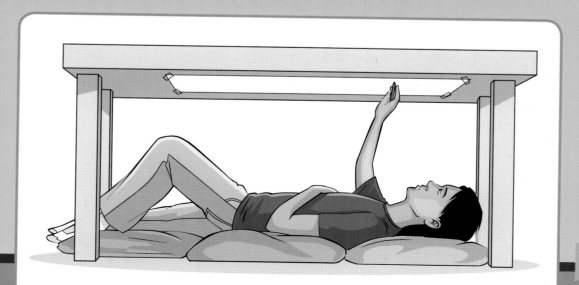

Later works

Michelangelo lived until he was 88 years old. He continued to work on massive sculptures until just a few weeks before his death.

The *Last Judgment*

More than 20 years after he had finished the Sistine ceiling, Michelangelo worked in the **chapel** again. This time he painted the *Last Judgment* on a huge wall. His painting shows Christ the judge sending people to heaven or hell.

The *Last Judgment* is very different from the cheerful scenes on the chapel ceiling. The painting seems to express Michelangelo's feelings of sadness as he grew older.

This hopeless figure comes from Michelangelo's *Last Judgment*.

Michelangelo's tomb

When he was 72 years old, Michelangelo started work on a sculpture for his own **tomb**. The subject he chose was a *Pietà* (Mary holding her dead son). He had carved this subject when he was young (see page 11), but his later carving was very different. It shows an old man supporting the body of Christ. This man is thought to be a self-portrait of Michelangelo.

Damaged masterpiece

Michelangelo never finished the carving for his tomb. The marble developed some cracks, and he lost his temper and smashed the work with his hammer. You can see the figure of Christ is missing one leg, and his arm has been mended.

The Florence *Pietà* was intended for Michelangelo's own tomb. Some people think it includes a self-portrait of the **sculptor** as an old man.

An all-round genius

Michelangelo was an outstanding painter and **sculptor**, but he also had other talents. He could design buildings and write beautiful love poems. In the last 20 years of his life, he composed many poems about death.

Amazing buildings

At the age of 86, Michelangelo designed a **dome** (a large, rounded roof) for St Peter's Church in Rome. The dome was built after his death. Today it is one of Rome's most famous sights.

Michelangelo's dome stands out proudly above the city of Rome.

Michelangelo also designed some buildings in Florence. He was the **architect** of the Medici **Chapel**. This was a very grand building made from grey and white marble. He also designed the Laurentian Library. Some of the library walls have blank **panels**, surrounded by marble frames. They look rather frightening, like a set of blocked-up windows and doors.

Look at the effect of the blank wall panels in the Laurentian Library.

Rothko and Michelangelo

In the 1950s, the American artist Mark Rothko visited Florence. He never forgot the panels in the Laurentian Library. Later, they inspired him to create the *Seagram* **Murals**. Rothko's murals look rather like dark, blocked-up windows. He said his murals were meant to be frightening, just like Michelangelo's blank panels.

After Michelangelo

After Michelangelo, sculpture and painting were never the same again. He showed that figures could be graceful but also filled with energy. He also taught artists to observe the human body carefully. Many artists who came after him studied his works, to help them learn more about their art.

Learning from Michelangelo

Michelangelo's work had a huge impact in the century following his death. The Italian painter Caravaggio created paintings that are filled with passion and movement, just like the work of Michelangelo (see page 16).

Sculptors also responded to Michelangelo. The great sculptor Bernini was inspired by Michelangelo's powerful carved figures.

Gian Lorenzo Bernini sculpted *Angel Kneeling With Hands at Heart* in 1673.

Michelangelo today

Michelangelo's art still makes a strong impression today. Art students make careful copies of his work. Companies use Michelangelo's images to sell their products, and **pavement artists** recreate his paintings on city streets. Every year, thousands of people travel to Florence and Rome in Italy to see Michelangelo's masterpieces for themselves.

Rodin and Michelangelo

The French sculptor Auguste Rodin worked in the late 1800s and early 1900s. Even though he worked in a modern style, he was still inspired by Michelangelo. Rodin especially admired Michelangelo's figures of men and boys.

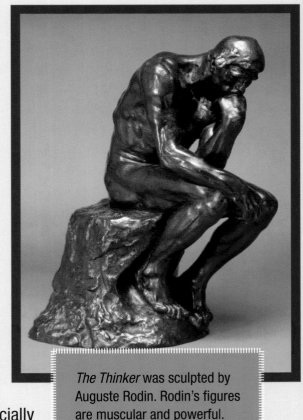

The Thinker was sculpted by Auguste Rodin. Rodin's figures are muscular and powerful.

Timeline

c.1350	The **Renaissance** begins in Italy.
1455	Johann Gutenberg produces the first printed book in Germany.
1475	Michelangelo is born in Caprese, Italy.
1487	The first European navigator sails around Africa.
1488	Michelangelo joins the **studio** of Ghirlandaio as a painter's apprentice.
1490	Michelangelo joins the sculpture school at the Medici Palace.
1492	Christopher Columbus reaches America. Lorenzo de Medici dies.
1499	Michelangelo completes the Rome *Pietà*.
1499	Amerigo Vespucci reaches South America.
1503	Leonardo starts painting the *Mona Lisa*.
1504	Michelangelo completes his statue of *David*.
1509	Henry VIII becomes king of England.
1512	Michelangelo finishes painting the ceiling of the Sistine **Chapel** in Rome, four years after he started it in 1508.
1521	Hernán Cortés conquers the Aztecs in Mexico.
1522	Ferdinand Magellan finished sailing around the world.

1524	Michelangelo designs the Laurentian Library.
1526	The Moghuls conquer northern India.
1532	The Incas of South America are conquered by Spanish soldiers.
1534	Jacques Cartier starts to explore eastern Canada.
1541	Michelangelo completes his painting the *Last Judgement*.
1547	Michelangelo begins the Florence *Pietà*. Ivan the Terrible becomes tsar of Russia.
1558	Elizabeth I becomes queen of England.
1561	Michelangelo designs the **dome** for St Peter's Church in Rome.
1564	Michelangelo dies, aged 88. William Shakespeare is born.

Glossary

3-D three dimensional. A 3-D shape has three dimensions (length, width, and depth).

architect someone who designs buildings

armour metal covering worn by soldiers to protect them in battle

chapel small church, where Christians worship

concentration very focused thinking

dignified calm, serious, and in control

dome large, rounded roof

independent free and not controlled by other people

merchant someone who trades goods

monk man who lives in a religious community and promises to serve God

mural painting on a wall

panel flat piece of material, such as marble or wood

patron someone who pays an artist to make works of art

pavement artist someone who draws pictures on pavements in return for money from passers-by

proportion size of one thing in relation to another thing

Renaissance rebirth of art, learning, and architecture that began in Italy around the 1350s until about 1600

Roman Catholic Church branch of the Christian Church, which is led by the Pope in Rome

sculptor artist who carves sculptures out of stone or wood

studio place where an artist works

tomb grave for an important person

Find out more

Books

Michelangelo, Philip Wilkinson (QED Publishing, 2006)

Michelangelo: The Young Artist Who Dreamed of Perfection, Philip Wilkinson (National Geographic Society, 2006)

Movements in Art: The Renaissance, Anne Fitzpatrick (Creative Education, 2005)

Websites

www.ibiblio.org/wm/paint/auth/michelangelo
This website presents some famous examples of Michelangelo's art.

www.wga.hu/bio/m/michelan/biograph.html
An introduction to the life and work of Michelangelo, with links to examples of his work.

www.casabuonarroti.it/english/e-home
The website of the Casa Buonarroti, a museum devoted to Michelangelo's work and life.

Places to see Michelangelo's art

Florence, Italy
Accademia Gallery (original of the statue of *David*)
Medici Chapel (sculptures)
Palazzo Vecchio (copy of the statue of *David*)
Uffizi Museum (paintings)

Rome, Italy
St. Peter's Church (architecture)
The Sistine Chapel (paintings)

London
British Museum (drawings)
Courtauld Institute of Art (drawings and sculptures)
National Gallery of Art (paintings)

Index